MAINE COON Cats

by Joanne Mattern

CAPSTONE PRESS
a capstone imprint

Edge Books are published by Capstone Press,
151 Good Counsel Drive, P.O. Box 669, Mankato, Minnesota 56002.
www.capstonepub.com

Books published by Capstone Press are manufactured with paper
containing at least 10 percent post-consumer waste.

Library of Congress Cataloging-in-Publication Data
Mattern, Joanne, 1963–
Maine coon cats / by Joanne Mattern.
    p. cm. —(Edge books. All about cats.)
Includes bibliographical references and index.
Summary: "Describes the history, physical features, temperament, and care of
    the Maine Coon cat breed"—Provided by publisher.
ISBN 978-1-4296-6631-2 (library binding)
1. Maine coon cat—Juvenile literature. I. Title.
SF449.M34M38 2011
636.8'3—dc22
                                                    2010032443

Editorial Credits

Connie R. Colwell and Carrie Braulick Sheely, editors; Heidi Thompson, designer;
    Wanda Winch, media researcher; Eric Manske, production specialist

Photo Credits

Barbara O'Brien, 5, 6; Capstone Press/Karon Dubke, 29, iStockphoto:
Constance McGuire, 10; Peter Arnold: Jean-Luc & Francoise Ziegler, 25;
Photo by Fiona Green, 23, Ron Kimball Stock: Ron Kimball Studios, 9,
15; Shutterstock: Dee Hunter, cover, Linn Currie, 11, 12, 18, 19, 21,
Ludmila Pankova, 17; Ulrike Schanz Photodesign & Animal Stock, 27

Printed in the United States of America in Stevens Point, Wisconsin.

092010   005934WZS11

TABLE OF CONTENTS

Chapter 1

GENTLE GIANTS

The Maine Coon is the largest native cat breed in North America. To go along with their large size, Maine Coons have big personalities. Their friendly, playful nature makes it easy to see why they're so popular. The Maine Coon's easygoing personality has even earned it a nickname—the "Gentle Giant" of the cat world.

In 2009 the Maine Coon was the third most popular breed in the Cat Fanciers' Association (CFA). The CFA is the world's largest cat registry.

LONGHAIRED BEAUTIES

Besides their personalities, Maine Coons are admired for their beauty. These cats have silky, long coats and a kind expression. In the 1860s, the classy appearance of Maine Coons made them popular in early U.S. cat shows.

breed—a certain kind of animal within an animal group; breed also means to mate and raise a certain kind of animal

registry—an organization that keeps track of the ancestry for cats of a certain breed

The Maine Coon's long, silky fur gives it an elegant look.

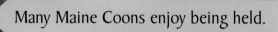

Many Maine Coons enjoy being held.

IS A MAINE COON RIGHT FOR YOU?

Maine Coons are good-natured cats. They make wonderful family pets, even for large families. They seem to enjoy being around children, dogs, and other cats.

Maine Coons also seem to enjoy being involved in their owners' activities. If you're reading a magazine or doing a crossword puzzle, you can expect your Maine Coon to be beside you.

Maine Coons are hardy cats and are generally easy to care for. But because they are a longhaired breed, Maine Coons need to be brushed weekly.

If the Maine Coon is right for you, the best place to buy a kitten is from a breeder. Most breeders take steps to be sure the kittens are healthy. Adoption is another way to find a Maine Coon. Animal shelters and breed rescue groups help match people with pets that need new, loving homes.

hardy—tough and able to survive in difficult conditions

Chapter 2

MAINE COON HISTORY

The Maine Coon is one of the oldest cat breeds in North America. The breed's long history has to do with its development. Most cat breeds are the result of careful breeding. Cat breeders select cats with desirable traits or qualities. Breeders then mate male and female cats that have these traits. Breeders hope that the resulting kittens will have the preferred characteristics.

The Maine Coon is considered a natural breed. A natural breed develops without interference from people. Because people didn't breed the Maine Coon, no one is certain how the breed came about. Several legends exist about this breed's history.

POPULAR LEGENDS

One common legend says the Maine Coon breed developed from wild cats mating with raccoons. This belief comes from Maine Coons' bushy tails and some Maine Coons' brown tabby coloring. But this story is false. It is impossible for cats to breed with raccoons.

legend—a story handed down from earlier times

tabby—having a striped coat

8

The brown tabby color pattern is very common in the Maine Coon breed.

Another legend says that Maine Coons descended from royal cats in France. In the 1790s, France was at war. Marie Antoinette was France's queen. She wanted to escape to North America during the war. The queen asked Samuel Clough to bring some of her valuable possessions to North America by ship. She planned to follow a short time later.

Marie Antoinette (seated) became queen of France in 1774.

Clough brought the queen's furniture, china, and six of her longhaired cats with him to Maine. But the queen never made it to Maine to claim her cats and possessions. She was killed during the war. Clough decided to keep the queen's cats in North America. According to the legend, these cats mated with native cats in North America, producing Maine Coons.

FACT: One legend says that Vikings brought relatives of the Maine Coon to North America. The Vikings traveled to North America from Europe in the late 900s.

Harsh living conditions probably led the Maine Coon to develop its sturdy frame.

THE REAL STORY

Today most people agree that Maine Coon cats first came to North America from foreign countries. Long ago, many foreign ships traveled to the northeastern coast of North America to trade. Ship captains often brought cats along on these voyages. The cats killed rats and mice on the ships.

These cats developed features that helped them handle difficult conditions on the ships. They had large, sturdy frames. They also developed long coats that kept them warm and dry in cold, wet weather.

Ship cats often wandered ashore in search of food when ships stopped in North America. Many of these cats stayed in North America when the ships sailed home. These foreign cats mated with shorthaired cats native to North America. This breeding produced Maine Coons.

GAINING POPULARITY

During the late 1800s, Maine Coons were popular at cat shows in Maine, Massachusetts, and New York. In 1895 a Maine Coon received the Best Cat award at the famous Madison Square Garden show in New York.

After 1895 Persian cats began to arrive in North America from Europe. More people wanted to own and breed Persians than Maine Coons. This change caused the number of Maine Coons in North America to decline.

But some breeders still admired Maine Coons. They worked hard to keep the breed alive. In 1975 the CFA recognized the Maine Coon as an official breed. By 1976 all North American cat registries recognized the breed. Over the next several years, Maine Coons won grand championship titles and other important awards at CFA shows.

FACT: The 1990-1991 CFA show season was a record-breaking one for Maine Coons. Three Maine Coons won National Winner titles.

After the 1970s, Maine Coons made a huge comeback as show cats.

15

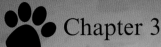 Chapter 3

BIG AND BUSHY-TAILED

Today most Maine Coons are household pets, and they no longer need to live on their own. But people still admire the unique features the Maine Coon naturally developed. From its large size to its square jaws, a Maine Coon has a look all its own.

Maine Coons can weigh as much as 20 pounds (9.1 kilograms). Male Maine Coons usually weigh between 13 and 18 pounds (5.9 and 8.2 kg). Females are slightly smaller. Most weigh between 8 and 12 pounds (3.6 and 5.4 kg).

Maine Coons have sturdy, rectangular bodies that have good proportion. Muscular legs and large feet support the cats' solid frames.

Maine Coons mature more slowly than most cat breeds. Maine Coons usually do not reach their full size until they are 3 to 5 years old. Most other cat breeds are fully grown at 1 year.

COATS

Maine Coons have long, thick, fluffy coats. The fur on their legs and undersides is especially long. The fur is shorter on their heads, shoulders, and backs. A Maine Coon's coat is silky to the touch.

proportion—the relation of one part to another; animals have good proportion when one body part doesn't seem too large or too small when compared to another

Many people think the square jaws and high cheekbones of Maine Coons give them a kind expression.

FACT: A Maine Coon's large feet help it walk over snow without sinking.

The length of Maine Coons' coats varies with the seasons. In winter their fur becomes thick and heavy. Winter coats can be 2 to 3 inches (5.1 to 7.6 centimeters) long. Maine Coons shed this longer fur during the spring and summer.

Maine Coons often have a **ruff** around their necks. They also have tufts of fur on the tips of their ears and between their toes.

ruff—a fringe or frill of long hairs growing around the neck of an animal

Ear tufts are common among longhaired breeds such as Maine Coons.

The Maine Coon's tail is often as long as its body.

TAIL

A Maine Coon's long, bushy tail is usually one of the first features people notice. The tail is wide at the base and tapers to a narrower point.

FACIAL FEATURES

Maine Coons have square jaws with high cheekbones. Their oval-shaped eyes are large and set wide apart. Eye color varies. It can be either one color or a mixture of colors. Green, gold, and copper eyes are common.

FACT: Maine Coons may wrap themselves in their bushy tails to keep warm.

COLORS

Maine Coons can have almost any coat color. These colors include black, blue, red, cream, silver, and brown.

Maine Coons can also have one of many patterns. Many are solid or tabby. Others have a dark color with patches of white. Calico Maine Coons are white with patches of red and black.

The CFA does not register Maine Coons with colors that don't occur naturally. These include the colorpoint markings found in Siamese and Himalayan cats. Cats with colorpoints have light-colored coats with darker fur on their ears, feet, face, and tail.

PERSONALITY

Maine Coons are curious and playful. They want to be involved in the activities going on around them. Adult Maine Coons often run and play as kittens do. The cats' playfulness is a great source of entertainment for their owners.

Maine Coons are also loyal and friendly. These traits have led some people to call them the "dogs of the cat world." Like dogs, Maine Coons seem to enjoy attention from their owners. These cats often can be found sitting near their owners. Many Maine Coons follow their owners from room to room.

Like other tabbies, red tabby Maine Coons have a marking that looks like an "M" on their foreheads.

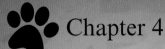

Chapter 4

CARING FOR A MAINE COON

Maine Coons are sturdy, strong cats. With good care, they can live 12 to 15 years.

Like other cats, Maine Coons should always be kept indoors. Letting a cat outdoors is dangerous. Cats that roam outdoors have greater risks of developing diseases than cats that are kept indoors. Outdoor cats also face dangers from cars and other animals.

FEEDING

A balanced, healthy diet keeps a Maine Coon looking and feeling its best. High-quality cat foods can be purchased at pet supply stores.

Some owners feed their cats dry food. This food usually is less expensive than other types of food. Dry food also can help keep cats' teeth clean. Other owners prefer to feed their cats moist, canned food. To keep it from spoiling, moist food should not be left out for more than one hour.

Cats need to drink water to stay healthy. They should always have a bowl of fresh, clean water available.

Dry food usually is formed into very small bite-size pieces so your cat can easily chew it.

LITTER BOXES

Cats get rid of bodily waste in their litter boxes. Be sure to clean the waste out of the box each day. Change the litter about every two weeks or whenever most of the litter is wet or lumpy. Cats are clean animals and may refuse to use a dirty litter box.

COAT GROOMING

Most cats do a good job of grooming their fur with their tongues. But some longhaired breeds such as the Maine Coon also need regular brushing. Brushing gets rid of loose hair and helps keep hairballs from forming.

Owners should brush Maine Coons once each week. Pure bristle brushes work best on Maine Coons. Combs work well on the thicker areas of the coat.

litter—small bits of clay or other material used to absorb the waste of cats and other animals

hairball—a ball of fur that lodges in a cat's stomach

DENTAL CARE

Cats need regular dental care to protect their teeth and gums from plaque. A buildup of germs on the teeth can cause tooth decay. You should brush your cat's teeth at least once a week. Use a special toothbrush made for cats or a soft cloth. Always use toothpaste made for cats. Toothpaste made for people can make cats sick.

Combs can help untangle mats in a Maine Coon's ruff.

NAIL CARE

Cats need their nails trimmed every few weeks. Nail trimming helps reduce damage if cats claw furniture. It also protects cats from infections caused by ingrown nails. You may choose to use a trimmer made for cats to make this job easier.

It is best to begin trimming a cat's nails when it is a kitten. The kitten will become used to having its nails trimmed as it grows older.

Some people take their cats to the veterinarian to be declawed. These permanent surgeries either remove part of the claw or keep a cat from **retracting** the claw. But declawing can cause cats pain after the surgeries. It also puts the cats at risk if they accidentally get outdoors. The cats are less able to hunt and defend themselves. For these reasons, the CFA and other organizations disapprove of declawing.

retract—to draw back in; cats can retract and extend their claws

EXERCISE

Maine Coons are playful cats. A variety of toys will help keep your Maine Coon from becoming bored. Many cats enjoy chasing small balls or playing with toy mice.

A scratching post can keep your cat from scratching on furniture.

 **FACT:** Some cats have more than five claws or extra toes. These cats are known as polydactyls. Maine Coons with extra toes are not allowed to be shown at CFA shows.

HEALTH CARE

Owners should take their cats to a veterinarian at least once each year. At these visits, your cat will receive any necessary vaccinations. The vet will also look for signs of health problems. Maine Coons are generally very healthy, but they may develop some health problems. Some Maine Coons suffer from hip dysplasia. The hip bones of an animal with this condition do not fit together properly. Hip dysplasia makes movement difficult.

Maine Coons are also prone to the **inherited** diseases cardiomyopathy and spinal muscular atrophy (SMA). Cardiomyopathy is a serious heart disease that causes the heart walls to thicken or stretch. SMA causes muscle weakness and can affect movement.

Owners who aren't planning to breed their cats should have them spayed or neutered by a vet. These surgeries make it impossible for cats to have kittens. Fewer unwanted kittens helps control the pet population. Spaying and neutering also helps keep your cat from developing certain types of cancer and other diseases.

Maine Coons make wonderful family pets. Their playful, friendly personalities give their owners unexpected reasons to smile day after day. With good care, owners can help their cats live long, healthy lives.

vaccination—a shot of medicine that protects animals from a disease

inherit—to receive a characteristic from parents

A Maine Coon that is well cared for can provide you with years of loving companionship.

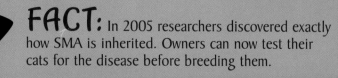

FACT: In 2005 researchers discovered exactly how SMA is inherited. Owners can now test their cats for the disease before breeding them.

GLOSSARY

breed (BREED)—a certain kind of animal within an animal group; breed also means to mate and raise a certain kind of animal

hairball (HAIR-bawl)—a ball of fur that lodges in a cat's stomach

hardy (HAR-dee)—able to survive in difficult conditions

inherit (in-HAYR-it)—to receive a characteristic from parents

legend (LEJ-uhnd)—a story handed down over time

litter (LIT-ur)—small bits of clay or other material used to absorb the waste of cats and other animals

plaque (PLAK)—the coating of food, saliva, and bacteria that forms on teeth and can cause tooth decay

proportion (pruh-POR-shuhn)—the relation of one part to another; animals have good proportion when a body part doesn't seem too large or too small when compared to another

registry (REH-juh-stree)—an organization that keeps track of the ancestry for cats of a certain breed

retract (ree-TRAKT)—to draw back in

ruff (RUHF)—long hairs growing around an animal's neck

tabby (TAB-ee)—having a striped coat

vaccination (vak-suh-NAY-shun)—a shot of medicine that protects animals from a disease

30

READ MORE

Mattern, Joanne. *Persian Cats.* All About Cats. Mankato, Minn.: Capstone Press, 2011.

Scheunemann, Pam. *Marvelous Maine Coons.* Cat Craze. Edina, Minn.: ABDO Pub., 2010.

Wilsdon, Christina. *Cats.* Amazing Animals. Pleasantville, N.Y.: Gareth Stevens Pub., 2009.

INTERNET SITES

FactHound offers a safe, fun way to find Internet sites related to this book. All of the sites on FactHound have been researched by our staff.

Here's all you do:

Visit *www.facthound.com*

Type in this code: 9781429666312

 **Super-cool stuff!** Check out projects, games and lots more at **www.capstonekids.com**

31

INDEX